SCHIZOPHRENIA

Causes, Symptoms, Signs, Diagnosis and Treatments

U.S. DEPARTMENT OF HEALTH AND HUMAN SERVICES, National Institutes of Health, National Institute of Mental Health, S. Smith - Illustrator

SCHIZOPHRENIA

Table of Contents

What is schizophrenia?

Schizophrenia is a chronic, severe, and disabling brain disorder that has been recognized throughout recorded history. It affects about 1 percent of Americans.1

People with schizophrenia may hear voices other people don't hear or they may believe that others are reading their minds, controlling their thoughts, or plotting to harm them. These experiences are terrifying and can cause fearfulness, withdrawal, or extreme agitation. People with schizophrenia may not make sense when they talk, may sit for hours without moving or talking much, or may seem perfectly fine until they talk about what they are really thinking. Because many people with schizophrenia have difficulty holding a job or caring for themselves, the burden on their families and society is significant as well.

Available treatments can relieve many of the disorder's symptoms, but most people who have schizophrenia must cope with some residual symptoms as long as they live. Nevertheless, this is a time of hope for people with schizophrenia and their families. Many people with the disorder now lead rewarding and meaningful lives in their communities. Researchers are developing more effective medications and using new research tools to understand the causes of schizophrenia and to find ways to prevent and treat it.

This brochure presents information on the symptoms of schizophrenia, when the symptoms appear, how the disease develops, current treatments, support for patients and their loved ones, and new directions in research.

What are the symptoms of schizophrenia?

The symptoms of schizophrenia fall into three broad categories:

• Positive symptoms are unusual thoughts or perceptions, including hallucinations, delusions, thought disorder, and disorders of movement.

• Negative symptoms represent a loss or a decrease in the ability to initiate plans, speak, express emotion, or find pleasure in everyday life. These symptoms are harder to recognize as part of the disorder and can be mistaken for laziness or depression.

• Cognitive symptoms (or cognitive deficits) are problems with attention, certain types of memory, and the executive functions that allow us to plan and organize. Cognitive deficits can also be difficult to recognize as part of the disorder but are the most disabling in terms of leading a normal life.

Positive symptoms
Positive symptoms are easy-to-spot behaviors not seen in healthy people and usually involve a loss of contact with reality. They include hallucinations, delusions, thought disorder,

and disorders of movement. Positive symptoms can come and go. Sometimes they are severe and at other times hardly noticeable, depending on whether the individual is receiving treatment.

Hallucinations. A hallucination is something a person sees, hears, smells, or feels that no one else can see, hear, smell, or feel. "Voices" are the most common type of hallucination in schizophrenia. Many people with the disorder hear voices that may comment on their behavior, order them to do things, warn them of impending danger, or talk to each other (usually about the patient).They may hear these voices for a long time before family and friends notice that something is wrong. Other types of hallucinations include seeing people or objects that are not there, smelling odors that no one else detects (although this can also be a symptom of certain brain tumors), and feeling things like invisible fingers touching their bodies when no one is near.

Delusions. Delusions are false personal beliefs that are not part of the person's culture and do not change, even when other people present proof that the beliefs are not true or logical. People with schizophrenia can have delusions that are quite bizarre, such as believing that neighbors can control their behavior with magnetic waves, people on television are directing special messages to them, or radio stations are broadcasting their thoughts aloud to others. They may also have delusions of grandeur and think they are famous historical figures. People with paranoid schizophrenia can believe that others are deliberately cheating, harassing, poisoning, spying upon, or plotting against them or the people they care about. These beliefs are called delusions of persecution.

Thought Disorder. People with schizophrenia often have unusual thought processes. One dramatic form is disorganized thinking, in which the person has difficulty organizing his or her thoughts or connecting them logically. Speech may be garbled or hard to understand. Another form is "thought blocking," in which the person stops abruptly in the middle of a thought. When asked why, the person may say that it felt as if the thought had been taken out of his or her head. Finally, the individual might make up unintelligible words, or "neologisms."

Disorders of Movement. People with schizophrenia can be clumsy and uncoordinated. They may also exhibit involuntary movements and may grimace or exhibit unusual mannerisms. They may repeat certain motions over and over or, in extreme cases, may become catatonic. Catatonia is a state of immobility and unresponsiveness. It was more common when treatment for schizophrenia was not available; fortunately, it is now rare.

Negative symptoms

The term "negative symptoms" refers to reductions in normal emotional and behavioral states. These include the following:

• flat affect (immobile facial expression, monotonous voice),

• lak of pleasure in everyday life,

• diminished ability to initiate and sustain planned activity, and

• speaking infrequently, even when forced to interact.

People with schizophrenia often neglect basic hygiene and need help with everyday activities. Because it is not as obvious that negative symptoms are part of a psychiatric illness, people with schizophrenia are often perceived as lazy and unwilling to better their lives.

Cognitive symptoms

Cognitive symptoms are subtle and are often detected only when neuropsychological tests are performed. They include the following:

• poor "executive functioning" (the ability to absorb and interpret information and make decisions based on that information),

• inabilty to sustain attention, and

• problems with "working memory" (the ability to keep recently learned information in mind and use it right away).

What are the symptoms of schizophrenia?

Cognitive impairments often interfere with the patient's ability to lead a normal life and earn a living. They can cause great emotional distress.

When does it start and who gets it?

Psychotic symptoms (such as hallucinations and delusions) usually emerge in men in their late teens and early 20s and in women in their mid-20s to early 30s. They seldom occur after age 45 and only rarely before puberty, although cases of schizophrenia in children as young as 5 have been reported. In adolescents, the first signs can include a change of friends, a drop in grades, sleep problems, and irritability. Because many normal adolescents exhibit these behaviors as well, a diagnosis can be difficult to make at this stage. In young people who go on to develop the disease, this is called the "prodromal" period.

Research has shown that schizophrenia affects men and women equally and occurs at similar rates in all ethnic groups around the world.

Are people with schizophrenia violent?

People with schizophrenia are not especially prone to violence and often prefer to be left alone. Studies show that if people have no record of criminal violence before they develop schizophrenia and are not substance abusers, they are unlikely to commit crimes after they become ill. Most violent crimes are not committed by people with schizophrenia, and most people with schizophrenia do not commit violent crimes. Substance abuse always increases violent behavior, regardless of the presence of schizophrenia (see sidebar). If someone with paranoid schizophrenia becomes violent, the violence is most often directed at family members and takes place at home.

What about suicide?

People with schizophrenia attempt suicide much more often than people in the general population. About 10 percent (especially young adult males) succeed. It is hard to predict which people with schizophrenia are prone to suicide, so if someone talks about or tries to commit suicide, professional help should be sought right away.

What about substance abuse?

Some people who abuse drugs show symptoms similar to those of schizophrenia, and people with schizophrenia may be mistaken for people who are high on drugs. While most researchers do not believe that substance abuse causes schizophrenia, people who have schizophrenia abuse alcohol and/or drugs more often than the general population.

Substance abuse can reduce the effectiveness of treatment for schizophrenia. Stimulants (such as amphetamines or cocaine), PCP, and marijuana may make the symptoms of schizophrenia worse, and substance abuse also makes it more likely that patients will not follow their treatment plan.

Schizophrenia and nicotine

The most common form of substance abuse in people with schizophrenia is an addiction to nicotine. People with schizophrenia are addicted to nicotine at three times the rate of the general population (75-90 percent vs. 25-30 percent).

Research has revealed that the relationship between smoking and schizophrenia is complex. People with schizophrenia seem to be driven to smoke, and researchers are exploring whether there is a biological basis for this need. In addition to its known health hazards, several studies have found that smoking interferes with the action of antipsychotic drugs. People with schizophrenia who smoke may need higher doses of their medication.

Quitting smoking may be especially difficult for people with schizophrenia since nicotine withdrawal may cause their psychotic symptoms to temporarily get worse. Smoking cessation strategies that include nicotine replacement methods may be better tolerated. Doctors who treat people with schizophrenia should carefully monitor their patient's response to antipsychotic medication if the patient decides to either start or stop smoking.

What causes schizophrenia?

Like many other illnesses, schizophrenia is believed to result from a combination of environmental and genetic factors. All the tools of modern science are being used to search for the causes of this disorder.

Can schizophrenia be inherited?

Scientists have long known that schizophrenia runs in families. It occurs in 1 percent of the general population but is seen in 10 percent of people with a first-degree relative (a parent, brother, or sister) with the disorder. People who have second-degree relatives (aunts, uncles, grandparents, or cousins) with the disease also develop schizophrenia more often than the general population. The identical twin of a person with schizophrenia is most at risk, with a 40 to 65 percent chance of developing the disorder.

Our genes are located on 23 pairs of chromosomes that are found in each cell. We inherit two copies of each gene, one from each parent. Several of these genes are thought to be associated with an increased risk of schizophrenia, but scientists believe that each gene has a very small effect and is not responsible for causing the disease by itself. It is still not possible to predict who will develop the disease by looking at genetic material.

Although there is a genetic risk for schizophrenia, it is not likely that genes alone are sufficient to cause the disorder. Interactions between genes and the environment are thought to be necessary for schizophrenia to develop. Many environmental factors have been suggested as risk factors, such as exposure to viruses or malnutrition in the womb, problems during birth, and psychosocial factors, like stressful environmental conditions.

Do people with schizophrenia have faulty brain chemistry?

It is likely that an imbalance in the complex, interrelated chemical reactions of the brain involving the neurotransmitters dopamine and glutamate (and possibly others) plays a role in schizophrenia. Neurotransmitters are substances that allow brain cells to communicate with one another. Basic knowledge about brain chemistry and its link to schizophrenia is expanding rapidly and is a promising area of research.

Do the brains of people with schizophrenia look different?

The brains of people with schizophrenia look a little different than the brains of healthy people, but the differences are small. Sometimes the fluid-filled cavities at the center of the brain, called ventricles, are larger in people with schizophrenia; overall gray matter volume is lower; and some areas of the brain have less or more metabolic activity. Microscopic studies of brain tissue after death have also revealed small changes in the distribution or characteristics of brain cells in people with schizophrenia. It appears that many of these changes were prenatal because they are not accompanied by glial cells, which are always present when a brain injury occurs after birth. One theory suggests that problems during brain development lead to faulty connections that lie dormant until puberty. The brain undergoes major changes during puberty, and these changes could trigger psychotic symptoms.

The only way to answer these questions is to conduct more research. Scientists in the United States and around the world are studying schizophrenia and trying to develop new ways to prevent and treat the disorder.

How is schizophrenia treated?

Because the causes of schizophrenia are still unknown, current treatments focus on eliminating the symptoms of the disease.

Antipsychotic medications

Antipsychotic medications have been available since the mid1950s. They effectively alleviate the positive symptoms of schizophrenia. While these drugs have greatly improved the lives of many patients, they do not cure schizophrenia.

Everyone responds differently to antipsychotic medication. Sometimes several different drugs must be tried before the right one is found. People with schizophrenia should work in partnership with their doctors to find the medications that control their symptoms best with the fewest side effects.

The older antipsychotic medications include chlorpromazine (Thorazine®), haloperidol (Haldol®), perphenazine (Etrafon®, Trilafon®), and fluphenzine (Prolixin®).The older medications can cause extrapyramidal side effects, such as rigidity, persistent muscle spasms, tremors, and restlessness.

In the 1990s, new drugs, called atypical antipsychotics, were developed that rarely produced these side effects. The first of these new drugs was clozapine (Clozaril®). It treats psychotic symptoms effectively even in people who do not respond to other medications, but it can produce a serious problem called agranulocytosis, a loss of the white blood cells that fight infection. Therefore, patients who take clozapine must have their white blood cell counts monitored every week or two. The inconvenience and cost of both the blood tests and the medication itself has made treatment with clozapine difficult for many people, but it is the drug of choice for those whose symptoms do not respond to the other antipsychotic medications, old or new.

Some of the drugs that were developed after clozapine was introduced—such as risperidone (Risperdal®), olanzapine (Zyprexa®), quetiapine (Seroquel®), sertindole (Serdolect®), and ziprasidone (Geodon®)—are effective and rarely produce extrapyramidal symptoms and do not cause agranulocytosis; but they can cause weight gain and metabolic changes associated with an increased risk of diabetes and high cholesterol.

People respond individually to antipsychotic medications, although agitation and hallucinations usually improve within days and delusions usually improve within a few weeks. Many people see substantial improvement in both types of symptoms by the sixth week of treatment. No one can tell beforehand exactly how a medication will affect a particular individual, and sometimes several medications must be tried before the right one is found.

When people first start to take atypical antipsychotics, they may become drowsy; experience dizziness when they change positions; have blurred vision; or develop a rapid heartbeat, menstrual problems, sensitivity to the sun, or skin rashes. Many of these symptoms will go away after the first days of treatment, but people who are taking atypical antipsychotics should not drive until they adjust to their new medication.

If people with schizophrenia become depressed, it may be necessary to add an antidepressant to their drug regimen.

A large clinical trial funded by the National Institute of Mental Health (NIMH), known as CATIE (Clinical Antipsychotic Trials of Intervention Effectiveness), compared the effectiveness and side effects of five antipsychotic medications—both new and older antipsychotics—that are used to treat people with schizophrenia. For more information on CATIE, visit http://www.nimh.nih.gov/healthinformation/catie.cfm.

Length of Treatment. Like diabetes or high blood pressure, schizophrenia is a chronic disorder that needs constant management. At the moment, it cannot be cured, but the rate of recurrence of psychotic episodes can be decreased significantly by staying on medication. Although responses vary from person to person, most people with schizophrenia need to take some type of medication for the rest of their lives as well as use other approaches, such as supportive therapy or rehabilitation.

Relapses occur most often when people with schizophrenia stop taking their antipsychotic medication because they feel better, or only take it occasionally because they forget or don't think taking it regularly is important. It is very important for people with schizophrenia to take their medication on a regular basis and for as long as their doctors recommend. If they do so, they will experience fewer psychotic symptoms.

No antipsychotic medication should be discontinued without talking to the doctor who prescribed it, and it should always be tapered off under a doctor's supervision rather than being stopped all at once.

There are a variety of reasons why people with schizophrenia do not adhere to treatment. If they don't believe they are ill, they may not think they need medication at all. If their thinking is too disorganized, they may not remember to take their medication every day. If they don't like the side effects of one medication, they may stop taking it without trying a different medication. Substance abuse can also interfere with treatment effectiveness. Doctors should ask patients how often they take their medication and be sensitive to a patient's request to change dosages or to try new medications to eliminate unwelcome side effects.

There are many strategies to help people with schizophrenia take their drugs regularly. Some medications are available in long-acting, injectable forms, which eliminate the need to take a pill every day. Medication calendars or pillboxes labeled with the days of the week can both help patients remember to take their medications and let caregivers know whether medication has been taken. Electronic timers on clocks or watches can be programmed to beep when people need to take their pills, and pairing medication with routine daily events, like meals, can help patients adhere to dosing schedules.

Medication Interactions. Antipsychotic medications can produce unpleasant or dangerous side effects when taken with certain other drugs. For this reason, the doctor who prescribes the antipsychotics should be told about all medications (over-the-counter and prescription) and all vitamins, minerals, and herbal supplements the patient takes. Alcohol or other drug use should also be discussed.

Psychosocial treatment

Numerous studies have found that psychosocial treatments can help patients who are already stabilized on antipsychotic medication deal with certain aspects of schizophrenia, such as difficulty with communication, motivation, self-care, work, and establishing and maintaining relationships with others. Learning and using coping mechanisms to address these problems allows people with schizophrenia to attend school, work, and socialize. Patients who receive regular psychosocial treatment also adhere better to their medication schedule and have fewer relapses and hospitalizations. A positive relationship with a therapist or a case manager gives the patient a reliable source of information, sympathy, encouragement, and hope, all of which are essential for managing the disease. The therapist can help patients better understand and adjust to living with schizophrenia by educating them about the causes of the disorder, common symptoms or problems they may experience, and the importance of staying on medications.

Illness Management Skills. People with schizophrenia can take an active role in managing their own illness. Once they learn basic facts about schizophrenia and the principles of schizophrenia treatment, they can make informed decisions about their care. If they are taught how to monitor the early warning signs of relapse and make a plan to respond to these signs, they can learn to prevent relapses. Patients can also be taught more effective coping skills to deal with persistent symptoms.

Integrated Treatment for Co-occurring Substance Abuse. Substance abuse is the most common co-occurring disorder in people with schizophrenia, but ordinary substance abuse treatment programs usually do not address this population's special needs. Integrating schizophrenia treatment programs and drug treatment programs produces better outcomes.

Rehabilitation. Rehabilitation emphasizes social and vocational training to help people with schizophrenia function more effectively in their communities. Because people with schizophrenia frequently become ill during the critical career-forming years of life (ages 18 to 35) and because the disease often interferes with normal cognitive functioning, most patients do not receive the training required for skilled work. Rehabilitation programs can include vocational counseling, job training, money management counseling, assistance in learning to use public transportation, and opportunities to practice social and workplace communication skills.

Family Education. Patients with schizophrenia are often discharged from the hospital into the care of their families, so it is important that family members know as much as possible about the disease to prevent relapses. Family members should be able to use different kinds of treatment adherence programs and have an arsenal of coping strategies and problem-solving skills to manage their ill relative effectively. Knowing where to find outpatient and family services that support people with schizophrenia and their caregivers is also valuable.

Cognitive Behavioral Therapy. Cognitive behavioral therapy is useful for patients with symptoms that persist even when they take medication. The cognitive therapist teaches people with schizophrenia how to test the reality of their thoughts and perceptions, how to "not listen" to their voices, and how to shake off the apathy that often immobilizes them. This treatment appears to be effective in reducing the severity of symptoms and decreasing the risk of relapse.

Self-Help Groups. Self-help groups for people with schizophrenia and their families are becoming increasingly common. Although professional therapists are not involved, the group members are a continuing source of mutual support and comfort for each other, which is also therapeutic. People in self-help groups know that others are facing the same problems they face and no longer feel isolated by their illness or the illness of their loved one. The networking that takes place in self-help groups can also generate social action. Families working together can advocate for research and more hospital and community treatment programs, and patients acting as a group may be able to draw public attention to the discriminations many people with mental illnesses still face in today's world.

Support groups and advocacy groups are excellent resources for people with many types of mental disorders

What is the role of the patient's support system?

Support for those with mental disorders can come from families, professional residential or day program caregivers, shelter operators, friends or roommates, professional case managers, or others in their communities or places of worship who are concerned about their welfare. There are many situations in which people with schizophrenia will need help from other people.

Getting Treatment. People with schizophrenia often resist treatment, believing that their delusions or hallucinations are real and psychiatric help is not required. If a crisis occurs, family and friends may need to take action to keep their loved one safe.

The issue of civil rights enters into any attempt to provide treatment. Laws protecting patients from involuntary commitment have become very strict, and trying to get help for someone who is mentally ill can be frustrating. These laws vary from state to state, but, generally, when people are dangerous to themselves or others because of mental illness and refuse to seek treatment, family members or friends may have to call the police to transport them to the hospital. In the emergency room, a mental health professional will assess the patient and determine whether a voluntary or involuntary admission is needed.

A person with mental illness who does not want treatment may hide strange behavior or ideas from a professional; therefore, family members and friends should ask to speak privately with the person conducting the patient's examination and explain what has been happening at home. The professional will then be able to question the patient and hear the patient's distorted thinking for themselves. Professionals must personally witness bizarre behavior and hear delusional thoughts before they can legally recommend commitment, and family and friends can give them the information they need to do so.

Caregiving. Ensuring that people with schizophrenia continue to get treatment and take their medication after they leave the hospital is also important. If patients stop taking their medication or stop going for follow-up appointments, their psychotic symptoms will return. If these symptoms become severe, they may become unable to care for their own basic needs for food, clothing, and shelter; they may neglect personal hygiene; and they may end up on the street or in jail, where they rarely receive the kind of help they need.

Family and friends can also help patients set realistic goals and regain their ability to function in the world. Each step toward these goals should be small enough to be attainable, and the patient should pursue them in an atmosphere of support. People with a mental illness who are pressured and criticized usually regress and their symptoms worsen. Telling them what they are doing right is the best way to help them move forward.

How should you respond when someone with schizophrenia makes statements that are strange or clearly false? Because these bizarre beliefs or hallucinations are real to the patient, it will not be useful to say they are wrong or imaginary. Going along with the delusions will not be helpful, either. It is best to calmly say that you see things differently than the patient does but that you acknowledge that everyone has the right to see things in his or her own way. Being respectful, supportive, and kind without tolerating dangerous or inappropriate behavior is the most helpful way to approach people with this disorder.

What is the outlook for the future?

The outlook for people with schizophrenia has improved over the last 30 years or so. Although there still is no cure, effective treatments have been developed, and many people with schizophrenia improve enough to lead independent, satisfying lives.

This is an exciting time for schizophrenia research. The explosion of knowledge in genetics, neuroscience, and behavioral research will enable a better understanding of the causes of the disorder, how to prevent it, and how to develop better treatments to allow those with schizophrenia to achieve their full potential.

How can a person participate in schizophrenia research?

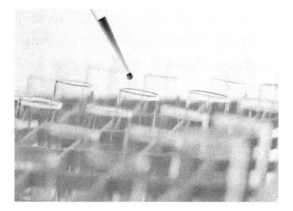

Scientists worldwide are studying schizophrenia so they will be able to develop new ways to prevent and treat the disorder. The only way it can be understood is for researchers to study the illness as it presents itself in those who suffer from it. There are many different kinds of studies. Some studies require that medication be changed; others, like genetic studies, require no change at all in medications.

To receive online information about federally and privately supported schizophrenia research, visit http://clinicaltrials.gov. This site describes an extensive list of studies being conducted across the United States. The information provided should be used in conjunction with advice from a health care professional.

NIMH conducts a Schizophrenia Research Program, which is located at the National Institute of Mental Health in Bethesda, Maryland. Travel assistance and study compensation are available for some studies. A list of outpatient and inpatient studies conducted at NIMH can be found at http://patientinfo.nimh.nih.gov. In addition, NIMH staff members can speak with you and help you determine whether their current studies are suitable for you or your family member. Simply call the toll free line at 1-888-674-6464. You can also indicate your interest in research participation by sending an email to Schizophrenia@intra.nimh.nih.gov. All calls remain confidential.

Addendum to Schizophrenia January 2007

Aripiprazole (Abilify) is another atypical antipsychotic medication used to treat the symptoms of schizophrenia and manic or mixed (manic and depressive) episodes of bipolar I disorder. Aripiprazole is in tablet and liquid form. An injectable form is used in the treatment of symptoms of agitation in schizophrenia and manic or mixed episodes of bipolar I disorder.

For More Information on Schizophrenia

1. Regier DA, Narrow WE, Rae DS, Manderscheid RW, Locke BZ, Goodwin FK. The de facto US mental and addictive disorders service system. Epidemiologic catchment area prospective 1-year prevalence rates of disorders and services. Arch Gen Psychiatry. 1993 Feb;50(2):85-94.

2. Catatonic Schizophrenia. (1992). The ICD-10 Classification of Mental and Behavioural Disorders: Clinical descriptions and diagnostic guidelines. Geneva, Switzerland:World Health Organization.

3. Mueser KT, McGurk SR. Schizophrenia. Lancet. 2004 Jun 19;363(9426):2063-72.

4. Meltzer HY, Alphs L, Green AI, Altamura AC, Anand R, Bertoldi A, Bourgeois M, Chouinard G, Islam MZ, Kane J, Krishnan R, Lindenmayer JP, Potkin S; International Suicide Prevention Trial Study Group. Clozapine treatment for suicidality in schizophrenia: International Suicide Prevention Trial (InterSePT). Arch Gen Psychiatry. 2003 Jan;60(1):82-91.

5. Meltzer HY, Baldessarini RJ. Reducing the risk for suicide in schizophrenia and affective disorders. J Clin Psychiatry. 2003 Sep;64(9):1122-9.

6. Jones RT & Benowitz NL. (2002).Therapeutics for Nicotine Addiction. In Davis KL, Charney D, Coyle JT & Nemeroff C (Eds.), Neuropsychopharmacology: The Fifth Generation of Progress (pp1533-1544). Nashville,TN:American College of

Neuropsychopharmacology.

7. Cardno AG, Gottesman II.Twin studies of schizophrenia: from bow-and-arrow concordances to star wars Mx and functional genomics. Am J Med Genet. 2000 Spring; 97(1):12-7.

8. Lieberman JA, Stroup TS, McEvoy JP, Swartz MS, Rosenheck RA, Perkins DO, Keefe RS, Davis SM, Davis CE, Lebowitz BD, Severe J, Hsiao JK; Clinical Antipsychotic Trials of Intervention Effectiveness (CATIE). Effectiveness of antipsychotic drugs in patients with chronic schizophrenia. N Engl J Med. 2005 Sep 22;353(12):1209-23.

For More Information on Schizophrenia

The National Library of Medicine, a service of the U.S. Library of Medicine and the National Institutes of Health, provides updated information on many health topics, including schizophrenia. It also lists mental health organizations that provide useful information. If you have Internet access, search for schizophrenia at http://medlineplus.gov.

EnEspanol http://medlineplus.gov/spanish/

Information from NIMH is available in multiple formats. You can browse online, download documents in PDF, and order paper brochures through the mail. If you would like to have NIMH publications, you can order them online at www.nimh.nih.gov. If you do not have Internet access and wish to have information that supplements this publication, please contact the NIMH Information Center at the numbers listed below.

For Further Information

National Institute of Mental Health Public Inquiries & Dissemination Branch 6001 Executive Boulevard
Room 8184, MSC 9663
Bethesda, MD 20892-9663
Phone: 301-443-5413 or
1-866-615-NIMH (6464) toll-free TTY: 301-443-8431
TTY: 866-415-8051
FAX: 301-443-4279
E-mail:nimhinfo@nih.gov
Web site:http://www.nimh.nih.gov
20 NATIONAL INSTITUTE OF MENTAL HEALTH

This publication is in the public domain and may be reproduced or copied without permission from the National Institute of Mental Health (NIMH). NIMH encourages you to reproduce this publication and use it in your efforts to improve public health. Citation of the NIMH as a source is appreciated. However, using government materials inappropriately can raise legal or ethical concerns, so we ask you to use these guidelines:

• NIMH does not endorse or recommend any commercial products, processes, or services and this publication may not be used for advertising or endorsement purposes.

• NIMH does not provide specific medical advice or treatment recommendations or referrals; these materials may not be used in a manner that has the appearance of such information.

• NIMH requests that Non-Federal organizations not alter this publication in a way that will jeopardize the integrity and "brand" when using the publication.

• Addition of Non-Federal Government logos and website links may not have the appearance of NIMH endorsement of any specific commercial products or services or medical treatments or services.

If you have questions regarding these guidelines and use of NIMH publications please contact the NIMH Information Center at 1-866-615-6464 or email at nimhinfo@nih.gov.

CPSIA information can be obtained
at www.ICGtesting.com
Printed in the USA
BVHW052151150523
664238BV00013B/360